BULLY GOAT GRUFF

Helyn Latimer

JELLY BEAN BOOKS · CARDIFF
2021

Editor: Shaun Russell
Editorial: Keren Williams

SECOND EDITION

Printed and bound in the UK by
Severn, Bristol Road, Gloucester, GL2 5EU

ISBN: 978-1-913637-25-5

Published by
Jelly Bean Books, Mackintosh House
136 Newport Road, Cardiff, CF24 1DJ
www.candyjarbooks.co.uk

For Dad.
Forever in my heart.

BULLY GOAT GRIFF REVIEWS

"This book made me laugh out loud. It is *really* funny." (Sam, 11)

"I couldn't put the book down." (Dan, 9)

"I just love this book. I love the characters. I love the story. My dad loved reading it too!" (Jessica, 8)

"This book is perfect for boys and girls." (Pam, librarian)

"A delightful book for 7–12 year olds and their parents, particularly if they appreciate Wales and the Welsh!" (Kath, bookstore assistant)

For more information about Helyn Latimer please visit her website: www.helynlatimerauthor.com

– CHAPTER ONE –

Bored Goat

Griff sniffed. Then he snorted. He was poised perfectly on a large rock with his two front hooves placed delicately, and with symmetrical precision, upon the highest point of the rock. His magnificent head was flung backwards and he gazed romantically up and into the deep, blue sky.

Interesting cloud formation today, he thought. The sharp tips of his huge, curved horns glinted in the sunlight. He carefully counted to five. Then slowly and deliberately raised his right hoof, maintaining the stunning pose for another five seconds, before suddenly performing a haughty and theatrical stamp of his right hoof. This always produced the exact, expected effect.

'Wow! Did you see the way he stamped then,

honey?' whispered a tourist.

'Yeah! He's one awesome goat! Get a photo!' replied another.

Griff turned toward all the cameras that were now pointed at him.

Pretty good crowd today, he thought. He then lowered his head slightly to show off his humungous horns, but also to make sure that the tourists could appreciate and feel threatened by his aggressive and manic stare.

'He's amazing! So big!' exclaimed an excited tourist.

Big? thought Griff. *Honestly, is that the best adjective they can come up with to describe my magnificence?*

'He's gigantic!'

A little better, thought Griff, though still disappointed.

'He's sensational!'

That'll do for today. Griff sighed. He enjoyed posing for all the daily tourists as they headed up the steep, Snowdonia mountain path, but it *was* becoming rather tedious. It was a few minutes 'duty' that he personally felt he ought to perform at eleven o'clock each morning, and being the most marvellous billy goat of the entire herd, he felt that it was only right to show off his magnificence.

Despite this, he had become tired and bored of all the effort – for what was, really, only a few moments of admiration each day. He needed a new challenge in his life.

He was about to turn and trot off arrogantly back down the slope, when an idea entered his head that would most certainly make his daily appearance feel more interesting and entertaining for all present.

He lowered his head further, began to stamp his right hoof with ever increasing agitation, and then he suddenly made a furious and daring dash towards the crowd! Screams of terror erupted as the crowd frantically dispersed into a multitude of directions.

Clouds of choking dust filled the mountainside. A walking boot flew high into the air, causing further panic as it descended and landed with a thud on the head of a dazed Italian tourist.

Meanwhile, Griff had abruptly halted, the tip of his left horn now frozen a mere millimetre away from a middle-aged, saggy bottom belonging to a bewildered American tourist. There were gasps of horror as everyone froze in fear all around. Griff's heart was pounding with excitement. He was such a daredevil!

However, it was clearly time for him to leave.

The show was over… Well, almost.

He slowly and delicately retreated from the saggy bottom, relishing in the final moments as his captivated audience stood around in silence, like stuffed animals with mouths gaping, too afraid to move a single muscle for fear of agitating the wild beast before them.

Griff gave a final snort, which of course set off further screams of terror and panic, before turning suddenly and setting off at an almighty gallop down the slope, and finally vanishing out of sight, leaving clouds of dust settling behind him.

– CHAPTER TWO –
Famous Goat

News of Griff's sudden and unexpected aggressive streak spread quickly through the Snowdonia mountain goat herd. From that day on, there wasn't a single goat who would dare to step into Griff's path or personal space. Whatever Griff wanted, Griff would get. The newest, sweetest clumps of lush, fresh grass were left unnibbled in case Griff fancied them for himself. The delicious carrots, cabbages, apples and pears offered by local children, and kind senior citizens, over the village stone wall at the bottom of the mountain, were always tasted by Griff first. Should Griff so wish to quench his thirst in the clear, running waters of the mountain streams, all other members of the goat herd would respectfully retreat and wait patiently until Griff felt sufficiently refreshed. Indeed, if there had been a troll lurking beneath any bridge that Griff had wished to trip trap over, then that troll would most certainly have remained respectfully silent under the bridge to avoid any issues of conflict to do with ownership or rights-of-way.

Griff assumed that all this respect and reverence was to do with his natural charm, wit, intelligence, stunning appearance, evident air of authority and, in general, his obvious magnificence. He had no doubt that the clever tourist taunting tactics that he had recently adopted had also helped to create this new, powerful goat-god-like image that he was relishing.

I am adored, he thought smugly as he gazed down upon a long line of fresh, new tourists in the distance, who had begun to weave their way up the steep mountain path. The number of visitors heading up the mountain each day had indeed doubled, if not quadrupled, since his first 'dramatic, exciting and heart-stopping performance' as he liked to think of it. Having continued to perform this incredible display at precisely eleven o'clock each morning, he just knew that all the tourists and, indeed, all the locals loved him for it.

It wasn't long before his image began to appear on tourist information leaflets, daring visitors to face their fears as they made their way up the mountain. Griff ornaments, toys and puppets, carvings, water colours and oil paintings and Griff-on-a-soap-on-a-rope soon filled up shop window displays and shelves, and sold like hot cakes.

Griff had become the most famous billy goat in Wales and beyond. Griff felt sensational. He was simply the best.

– CHAPTER THREE –

Bully Goat

F*ame is fantastic,* thought Griff as he nibbled on an enormous piece of cake. It had been hurled in his direction over the stone wall one afternoon by a generous five-year-old boy who was walking home with his mother having just enjoyed a friend's birthday party in the village hall. The boy had run ahead, leaving his mother a few hundred metres further down along the path. He had somehow managed to climb up onto the stone wall, clutching the string tied to a bright red balloon in one hand and the unwanted birthday cake in the other. He didn't like cake and thought that the goats might enjoy it instead.

'Dacw Griff, Mammy!' ('There's Griff, Mummy!') shouted little Sioni Siencyns, eyes wide-open with

excitement. (*'Sioni Siencyns'* is pronounced 'Shonee Shenkins'. If you place more emphasis on the first syllables then you will sound very Welsh indeed.)

'Bydd yn ofalus, cariad! Mae Griff yn beryglus iawn!' ('Be careful, love! Griff is very dangerous!') warned the boy's mother, now quickening her pace up the path, grateful that the old, stone wall served as a sturdy barrier between her precious child on one side and the wild, unpredictable beast on the other. Griff gave a loud snort and then posed with his meanest, fiercest (albeit cake-smothered) expression, much to the child's delight, and to the mother's alarm.

'Tyrd i lawr rwan, cariad,' ('Come down now, love.') warned little Sioni's mother, who was now becoming very worried. She had still not quite managed to catch up with little Sioni, and the child was now leaning precariously over the wall, waving at Griff with one hand, but still holding on tight to the string of the bright red balloon in the other. The huge billy goat was no more than a few metres away from the wall that little Sioni Siencyns was now

dangerously dangling over.

'Dw i eisiau gweld Griff!' ('I want to see Griff!') shouted the excited boy. Griff was aware of the mother's anxiety as she huffed and puffed her way closer up the path, and he could not resist being a little mischievous. He gulped down the rest of the cake and then took a few delicate steps towards little Sioni.

'Wyt ti'n hoffi'r deisen, Griff?' ('Do you like the cake, Griff?') said the boy, his face beaming. Griff stood directly in front of little Sioni, their faces only inches apart. Little Sioni Siencyns wobbled as a stone slipped away from beneath his foot. His priority was to save his precious balloon, so he quickly grabbed the balloon's string with both hands… and then fell.

'Sioni!' screamed his mother in terror. She had just made it in time to grab the back of her son's trousers and pants to stop him falling any further over the wall, where the mighty goat now stood looming over the child.

For about five seconds absolutely nothing happened. The mother stood open-mouthed, preparing to make the most excruciatingly loud scream imaginable while little Sioni smiled silently and stared deeply into Griff's hypnotic blue eye. Griff's other eye was brown, but it was the rectangular pupils of Griff's eyes that little Sioni found so interesting in those brief seconds of wonder.

Griff's attention over those five seconds, however, was fixed upon the bright, red balloon. Griff had often seen groups of young children racing out of the village hall, usually on Saturdays or Sundays, holding onto the string of their balloons with joy and happiness. Sometimes a child would let go of the string and the balloon floated up high into the sky until it was out of sight. This was usually followed with howls of despair and floods of tears as the unhappy child watched their beloved balloon float away forever. Griff often wondered where all the balloons went. Did they all meet up together somewhere far away and have great big balloon parties in the sky?

Griff also knew that sometimes, something else happened to the balloons, that was even more astonishing. They could sometimes simply vanish with a bang. When this happened, there were often howls of laughter and it was funny… but not always. This was an opportunity not to be missed. Griff could not resist. Griff was certain that little Sioni Siencyns would laugh because it would be so funny. Griff knew what had to be done. He leaned his head to one side and stuck the tip of his horn into the balloon.

There was a sudden, almighty bang and the balloon vanished as if by magic. Griff was delighted. It was so funny and amazing. He had made the balloon disappear! Now he was not only magnificent, but he was also magnificently magical. He waited for little Sioni to laugh. Little Sioni did not laugh. Little Sioni did not think it was funny. Little Sioni was devastated. As his mother let out the most excruciatingly loud scream imaginable, so too did little Sioni. It really hurt Griff's ears and he quickly backed away in surprise. Sioni's mother stopped screaming, much to Griff's relief. She pulled Sioni off the wall towards her and held him tightly.

'Bwli ydach chi!' ('You're a bully!') she shouted, and then turned and hurried away with the wailing child in her arms, leaving Griff standing alone the other side of the wall, feeling surprised but also rather proud of himself. He'd always wanted to make a balloon disappear and he couldn't wait for the next opportunity.

– CHAPTER FOUR –
Angry Goat

From that day on Griff noticed that the other mountain goats kept their distance. In fact, they never dared to go anywhere near him. He still got everything he wanted when he wanted, but it seemed to be more out of fear than respect and adoration. There was no doubt about it; he was avoided like a verruca.

There was one goat, however, who never seemed far away. Kev the Kid was small and skinny, and he had been following Griff like a shadow ever since… well, Griff wasn't quite sure how long Kev the Kid had been hanging around him. Perhaps he had always followed Griff? Maybe it was only *now* that Griff noticed him in particular, as there were simply no other goats anywhere near him?

Kev was just a kid, but he was beginning to irritate Griff no end, especially when he followed Griff up the mountain just before his eleven o'clock display each morning. Griff began to feel jealous when Kev got some of the attention from locals and visitors because he was so small and annoyingly cute.

'Awww. Look at that tiny one!' the tourists would say. 'He's so cute. Get a photo honey!' Griff could scarcely believe anyone could take any interest in such a skinny, insignificant bundle of skin, bones and scraggy hair on four legs. Kev didn't even have much in the way of horns. They were mere silly bumps on his head.

One day Griff had enough. It was ten to eleven in the morning and as Griff began to head up the mountain to perform his duty and pose for the tourists, that puny little goat began to follow him again. Griff stopped suddenly and turned back sharply and stared at Kev. He stamped his foot threateningly to warn Kev to back off or else. No one had the right to steal the limelight off Griff. This was his big moment each day and he wasn't going to let a kid like Kev spoil it.

Kev was fascinated by Griff. He had never seen such an amazing goat. Bully Goat Griff, as he was now known, was so incredible, so strong, so magnificent, so superior, so astonishing… but also so arrogant, so selfish and so alone.

He watched Griff every morning posing for the tourists and showing off and becoming more and more famous… and more and more arrogant and selfish. Kev watched Griff take more than his fair share of lush, green grass and tasty titbits offered by the locals, while the other goats rolled their eyes and shook their heads. He knew Griff was heading for trouble. Kev had watched the incident with Sioni Siencyns and the balloon. The locals stopped offering treats to any of the goats over the wall, and it was clearly Griff's fault.

In fact, there was only one local left who still liked to feed the goats. She was a dear, sweet elderly lady who lived in a cottage at the bottom of the mountain, and she continued to offer the goats tasty apples and pears from the trees in her garden. All the goats believed that she was either 'socially distant' from other members of her village community (and possibly a bit deaf) and therefore had not heard about how dangerous Griff had become, or she was so nutty about goats that she didn't care about the risks involved in getting so close to them all, especially Bully Goat Griff. Perhaps though, she was just a really kind and forgiving person, and decided that even naughty, nasty bully goats like Griff needed to be shown kindness and love?

Kev was kind. He didn't like the thought of any goat being lonely. He wanted to help Griff and show Griff that being a bully was bad. It was bad for everyone and it was bad for Griff. He wasn't sure how to approach him about this, and just ended up following him around, hoping that eventually Griff would notice him and take note of how a goat should behave. If Kev the Kid went up to all the visitors and gently bleated and politely nibbled on any food offered, then he could teach Griff that this sort of behaviour was far better than rushing at them and threatening them and frightening them.

He began to follow Griff every morning up to the rock, and each time he followed a little more closely behind. One morning, Kev the Kid got a little too close and he wasn't surprised when Griff suddenly stopped and turned in his tracks to face Kev with a manic stare.

Griff stamped a hoof menacingly. Usually this was all that was required to make any goat back off. He waited for Kev to do the sensible thing and turn away quickly. Kev, however, did not move. This was the bravest moment in Kev's entire life. He was on an important and determined mission to help Griff and he needed Griff to understand that he was not afraid and would not be bullied.

Griff was astonished. Was this scrawny little kid crazy? Didn't he know that Bully Goat Griff was the most important and most magnificent of all goats?

Poor kid, Griff finally thought. *I expect he's frozen to the spot utterly scared out of his wits unable to move. I'll ignore him and carry on. It's almost eleven o'clock.*

Griff turned and continued up the path and

leaped up onto the large, flat rock to adopt his usual magnificent pose, with his feet together and his head turned up to the sky. The tourists began to murmur with excitement.

'There he is, honey!' whispered a tourist. 'Didn't I tell you that we'd see him if we came up the mountain at eleven o'clock?'

'Oh yes! He's utterly adorable!

Griff was a bit surprised. He wasn't usually called 'adorable', but he liked it.

They really do love me. He beamed smugly. It was time for him to raise his right hoof to perfect that 'adorable' image.

'*Oh là là.* He's coming closer. *Très bien!*' exclaimed a French tourist.

I'm just raising my hoof, thought Griff. *But I'll be moving* very *close to you all in a few seconds.*

'Can I feed him, Mama?'

'Yes, of course, darling. Offer him your apple.'

Griff snorted, still gazing up at the sky.

Feed me? Are they mad? Surely they know what I'm about to do next? Griff decided it was time. He brought his right hoof down with a thud, and waited for the crowd to gasp in terror and begin screaming.

Instead, however, all he heard were gentle waves of 'Oooooh' and 'Ahhhhhhhh' and things like, 'How sweet!' and 'He's so gentle...' and 'He's the loveliest goat ever.'

Griff was confused. This wasn't the usual response to his fearful presence. He tried to raise his hoof, but he just wasn't focused enough to stamp it again. Something wasn't right. Why weren't all the tourists screaming and running away from him?

He lowered his head and turned towards the crowd, preparing to stare aggressively but discovered, to his utter disbelief, that not a single tourist was even looking at him. In fact, they were completely ignoring him. It was as if he didn't exist! Something was very wrong.

Then he realised what was going on. All eyes were fixed on Kev the Kid. There he was, lapping up all the attention and love and adoration that belonged to Griff. There he was being fed and patted by children and adults. There he was having his photo taken what appeared to be a million times!

Griff was furious. He felt a rage welling up deep inside him. How dare that puny kid steal his show! He couldn't bear all the 'cooing' a moment longer. A surge of anger overcame him and he exploded! He suddenly dashed, head down towards Kev the Kid!

'It's that horrible Bully Goat Griff!' somebody yelled. 'Run!' Everybody screamed and ran. Griff wasn't interested in scaring the tourists anymore. He just wanted to show that annoying little goat who was boss.

Kev didn't hang around a second more than

necessary. Kev was quick. He darted out of the way of Griff's sharp horns and escaped within a millimetre of his life! By the time Griff had rushed past him, slowed to turn and then straightened up for the next lunge, Kev was galloping down the mountain slope as fast as his tiny legs could carry him.

– CHAPTER FIVE –
Belittled Goat

It was going to be another pleasant and warm day in Snowdonia. (Yes, believe it or not, the sun does frequently shine in Snowdonia.)

At eleven o'clock every morning Mrs Evans-Williams-Jenkins-Jones would sit down in her garden and enjoy a nice cup of tea with a slice of homemade cake.

The sweet, elderly lady came out through the door of her quaint little cottage (yes – it *did* have roses growing around the door) and carefully placed the tray on the garden table. She always used her best porcelain tea set for her elevenses. Tea tasted so much better when it was poured out of a porcelain tea pot and into a porcelain tea cup that was placed upon a porcelain saucer.

She sat down and poured herself a cup of tea. She smiled and gazed up at the stunning mountain view that she enjoyed every day. As she picked up a fork, ready to delve into the delights of her freshly baked carrot cake, she heard the distant sound of tourists screaming halfway up the mountain. Mrs Evans-Williams-Jenkins-Jones had very good hearing.

'Ah, that'll be Griff up to his usual tricks with the tourists,' she said as she chuckled to herself. She loved all of the goats and all of the goats loved her. Each one had a unique character. She had given them all their names. There were the nanny goats: Prancing Poppy, Joyful Joy, Voracious Violet, Lovely Lily, Delicate Dew Drop, Sweet Pea, Precious Petal, Hairy Mary, Stunning Sylvia, Peculiar Petunia, Cautious Cerys, Merry Megan, to name but a few.

Then there were the billy goats: Adorable Alan, Tickly Terence, Ravenous Rory, Chuckling Charlie, Finest Fred, Lippy Lewis, Galivanting Gareth, Dancing Dafydd, Riotous Rhys, Happy Hywel, Grumpy Griff and Kev the Kid… to name but a few.

All were welcome to enter her garden and enjoy a feast of delicious freshly picked apples and pears and vegetables that she placed in a basket on her doorstep every afternoon. Her garden gate was always left wide open for the goats. She had been advised by the local police to close and lock the gate at all times after a thief made off with her small garden pagoda a few weeks previously, but such was her kindness and fondness for the goats that she didn't want to lock them out. She looked forward to their regular afternoon visits.

She was just about to place a piece of carrot cake on her fork when one of the smaller billy goats came dashing into the garden at top speed. He stopped suddenly in front of her to avoid running headlong into the table and stood quivering in the centre of a bare, square patch of earth where her missing garden pagoda had once been placed. Mrs Evans-Williams-Jenkins-Jones was startled for a moment.

'Goodness me, Kev. You made me jump! I'm afraid you're a little early. It's only just gone eleven o'clock and I haven't prepared the fruit and vegetables yet. You'll have to wait. There's a good goat.'

Kev stopped quivering. Somehow, Mrs Evans-Williams-Jenkins-Jones always made him feel safe and relaxed. He bleated softly and put his head to the side to look as cute and adorable as possible.

'Oh, go on then. Have a piece of carrot cake.' A piece of warm, moist carrot cake was flicked to the ground and Kev nibbled on it politely. It was heavenly. But, he knew that any second this blissful, beautiful, peaceful moment was about to be shattered, and so he made the most of it by polishing off the last few crumbs left on the ground.

About three seconds later, Griff came barging through the garden gate at full speed. Kev jumped sideways. Griff tried to stop but a large goat galloping at full speed is a difficult thing to stop. He went crashing into the table. Teapot, tea cup, saucer, plate and cake all flew high up into the air and seemed to fall in slow motion

down...

down...

down...

as Kev and Griff watched in horror waiting for the inevitable crash. They were aware that this was the kind lady's best porcelain and that it was about to be smashed to smithereens.

Now Mrs Evans-Williams-Jenkins-Jones may have been elderly, but she was also incredibly nimble and flexible. Within the time it took for everything to be flung up into the air she had swiftly managed to position herself directly beneath the descending pot and cup, saucer and plate. She caught the teapot in her right hand, the plate in her left hand, the saucer in her teeth and successfully caught the cup by its handle on her right toe. It was a good job she was wearing sandals and it was also fortunate that she had very long toes.

She placed the porcelain down carefully on her chair and then picked up the upturned table and set it back in place. She then carried the now empty teapot back indoors mumbling,

'Goats, eh? Naughty, Griff. I'll have to make another pot of tea now.'

Kev looked at the cake all over the ground and decided to help Mrs Evans-Williams-Jenkins-Jones to clear it up by eating every last bit he could find. He looked around for Griff. Where was he? He seemed to have vanished.

Then he noticed a greyish bottom with a flicking tail sticking out of one of Mrs Evans-Williams-Jenkins-Jones' blueberry bushes. Kev began to back out of the garden slowly and silently as he watched Griff trying to dislodge himself from the bush. He was hindered by his huge horns and it was a good five minutes before he finally managed to free himself.

Griff looked around for Kev the Kid, but realised he must have escaped out of the garden. He was still fuming with rage. He had lost everything because of that irritating, scrawny, puny little goat. He had lost his admiring tourist fan club, his job, his dignity and indeed his whole purpose in life, which was to look and be utterly cool and superior and magnificent at all times and in all places! Griff stood in the garden shaking with anger and rage and frustration.

'What are you snorting about, silly billy?' asked Mrs Evans-Williams-Jenkins-Jones as she re-emerged from the cottage with a fresh pot of tea and placed it on the table.

Kev was still lurking just outside the garden and he peeked his head around the gate. By this time, a fairly large gathering of goats had appeared at the bottom of the mountain and were peering over the garden wall to find out what all the noise was about. Mrs Evans-Williams-Jenkins-Jones went back inside and appeared once more with more cake on a plate.

'Oh, my fork has gone,' she said. 'Ah, there it is.' She leaned down to pick it up off the ground.

In that instant Griff lost all sense of reason. All he could see in front of him was Mrs Evans-Williams-Jenkins-Jones' frilly, laced knickers.

His only thought for a moment was, *Shall I butt the butt?* He needed to regain his dignity and leadership and power. All the other goats were watching. Kev was watching. This needed to be done. He would show them all who was the boss.

He put his head down and raced towards the frilly, laced bottom and to all the goats' horror Bully

Goat Griff butted Mrs Evans-Williams-Jenkins-Jones in the rear. She was slight and light and was flung high into the air. Fortunately she had been a gymnast in her youth, and she was still able to perform three incredible somersaults in the air before daintily descending and landing on the ground, perfectly central within the square patch of earth where her garden pagoda had once been placed. This time, she lost her patience.

'You're such a haughty and naughty goat. My posterior will be sore for days! Don't *ever* expect any more apples from me, young man! How could I ever trust you again? In fact, I shan't trust any of you goats again! None of you may take any more of my delicious apples, nor any of my voluptuous vegetables ever, **EVER** again!'

Griff was about to sneer mischievously, having expected her to possibly be a bit upset, but then her face, quite suddenly and alarmingly, went extremely red as she unexpectedly exploded with anger.

'I'm going to have the wall around my cottage built up higher to keep all of you slobbering, grovelling, ghastly, nasty, spiteful, frightful, monstrous mountain goats out of my gorgeous garden FOREVER!' Griff cautiously backed out of the garden gate just before she slammed it in his startled face.

With the rant over, Mrs Evans-Williams-Jenkins-Jones gathered up her precious porcelain and turned her tear-stained face away. With a final, 'Humph!' of disgust, she trotted off back down her garden path and viciously booted the door to the cottage open. She marched angrily inside, turned and gave Griff the most terrifying glare imaginable, and then, in the most roaring of rages, she karate kicked the door shut behind her.

Griff and three other quivering goats that had dared to remain and witness the whole incident, stood stunned and silent on the other side of the garden gate. The remaining three goats then nervously, cautiously and wisely retreated, afraid of what might happen next. Kev was long gone. Griff was left alone. He was too astonished to move. For the first time ever, in his whole selfish, spiteful and arrogant life, Bully Goat Griff felt… belittled.

– CHAPTER SIX –
Lovely Goat Major

Goat Major Morgan wiped one last tear away. It had been four weeks now since the sad passing of Gethin the Goat Mascot of the Royal Taff Regiment, but to Goat Major Morgan, it had felt like a lifetime without him.

Morgan and Gethin had been the best of buddies for the past ten years. Having selected Gethin himself as the most promising new goat mascot to be found in the whole of Snowdonia, Goat Major Morgan had then trained him with endless patience and gentleness for six months.

Gethin even had his own fan club and received thousands of letters from children all over Wales asking for his photo and hoof print. He had been the perfect goat mascot. He had loved every moment of his military mascot career, especially all the cheering and clapping and happy, excited faces of the crowds. His behaviour had been impeccable on and off parade. He had been the most obedient and good natured of all goat mascots.

Goat Major Morgan had adored caring for him and preparing him for all those special, happy occasions. Even in his declining years, Gethin had continued to perform his duty no matter how tired he may have felt. Goat Major Morgan knew that it was all getting a bit too much for Gethin in the end, and it was agreed that poor, old Gethin ought to be retired. His retirement only lasted a few days however as he passed peacefully away in his sleep one night with a smile on his face, having not long polished off a delicious baleful of fresh hay.

Goat Major Morgan now stood alone in Gethin's pen, having just finished sweeping it for the tenth time that week, as he simply couldn't get out of the habit. He gazed at the gleaming halter with brass buckles hanging on the hook and then patted the beautifully embroidered robe that hung on the wall. He took the shiny silver headdress off its hook and gave it a final rub with a cloth before carefully replacing it.

He had been summoned to Colonel Cadwaladr's office and couldn't be late. Goat Major Morgan turned to go. 'Oh, Gethin,' he said with a sigh. 'You can never be replaced.'

'Right! Gethin needs to be replaced!' ordered Colonel Cadwaladr the moment Goat Major Morgan entered his office.

'But, that's impossible, sir.' Goat Major Morgan

stuttered. 'Gethin can never be replaced.'

'Now listen to me, Goat Major, you've had long enough to get over Gethin. The Queen has been informed that Gethin is...' Goat Major Morgan stifled a grief-stricken gasp and the colonel rethought his sentence. 'Er... that Gethin is... er... sadly no longer with us. We need a new goat mascot as soon as possible. We have sought her majesty's permission to commission.'

'Permission to commission?' asked Goat Major Morgan.

'Yes, her permission to commission a new acquisition.'

'Her permission to commission a new acquisition?'

'That's right,' replied Colonel Cadwaladr impatiently. 'Do you have any opposition to such a commission of a new acquisition?'

'Am I in a position to have opposition to the commission of a new acquisition?' asked Goat Major Morgan. 'Or is that your final decision?' The colonel's moustache began to quiver. He took a deep breath and then began...

'I am stating with precision that it is indeed my

decision that her majesty's permission to commission a new acquisition should have no opposition and in recognition of this position and to maintain our long tradition, a necessary addition shall be made.'

Colonel Cadwaladr had spent several years studying and learning lots of lovely, long words and he relished any opportunity to use them, even if it meant that no one actually understood a word he was saying. Goat Major Morgan, however, always understood everything Colonel Cadwaladr said. You could say it was just intuition.

'You want me to find a new goat mascot then?' he asked.

'Yes!' replied the colonel. 'As soon as possible! Scour Snowdonia if you must! Find us a suitable goat mascot and get it trained up before the next Wales versus England match at the Principality Stadium!' That didn't give Goat Major Morgan long at all. It only gave him five months. It usually took six months to train up a goat mascot and that was only if the new goat behaved itself and was willing to learn quickly. This was important though. The Royal Taff Regiment needed a new goat mascot.

'Very well, Colonel Cadwaladr. I shall find a new goat mascot, but it may take time. It will need to be the right goat for the job. It won't be easy to find another goat as good as Gethin.'

'Have one found, trained and ready in time! That's an order! Off you go. Thank you. Dismissed!'

Goat Major Morgan returned to Gethin's pen. He had mourned for Gethin but now he needed to move on. He took the photo that he had kept of himself with Gethin meeting the Queen out of his pocket and smiled at it. He then tucked it away safely back into his pocket, along with all the happy memories, and set out on a new journey to find his next best friend.

– CHAPTER SEVEN–

Lonely Goat

Being famous had been wonderful. Being infamous, however, wasn't quite as good. Griff still maintained his respect and rank, and he was no doubt the commanding officer of the Snowdonia mountain goat herd. No other goat ever dared to step into his path. No other goat ever dared to go anywhere near him. He was always alone.

Kev the Kid had stopped following him up to the rock, so at least Griff could continue to perform his duty at eleven o'clock each morning without distraction.

A strong wooden fence though had been put in place to keep the tourists safe, close to the large rock where he always appeared and posed, and this rather spoilt all the action. News had spread fast about what had happened to poor Mrs Evans-Williams-Jenkins-Jones and no one was taking any chances. The tourists' reactions had become more subdued. They gazed upon Bully Goat Griff in awe and fascination and fear, but the adoration he had once enjoyed seemed to have disappeared.

It was strange not being liked. Griff wanted to be liked and loved, like everyone else did. All the other goats spent time together. They really liked being with each other but none of them wanted to be with Griff.

Griff began to feel lonely. He was so lonely that he even began to look around for Kev the Kid. Griff secretly wished that Kev was still following him and stealing his limelight, just so that he could get annoyed with him. At least that would have been some connection with another member of the herd.

I suppose this is what it's like at the top, thought Griff on another lonely afternoon. *It's a lonely place but someone has to be boss.* He gazed down the mountain side at all the grazing goats. *They need me. I'm incredibly important. They just don't appreciate me.*

He decided to wander down to the village. It was Saturday so maybe there would be cake. When he arrived at the wall close to the village hall, he discovered that a new sign had been put up. 'Do not feed the goats.' There would be no cake today, or ever again.

I wonder why? thought Griff, very disappointed.

Still, there was always Mrs Evans-Williams-Jenkins-Jones and her fruit and vegetable basket. When he reached her garden wall though, he couldn't believe his eyes. The wall had grown so high that even Griff could no longer peek over it. He trotted over to the gate. That too had grown taller and was firmly locked.

Oh no, thought Griff. *It must be because of that annoying, selfish thief who stole her pagoda.*

Griff felt lost and unhappy. His world was changing. He needed a new challenge in his life. A piece of newspaper fluttered above his head, caught up in a breeze. It then floated gently down and came to a rest at his feet.

It was the front page of the Snowdonia Weekly News. Griff's eye was caught by the photo of a magnificent goat mascot, wearing a splendid robe and silver headdress. He was standing next to a young man dressed in a smart army uniform who was talking to the Queen! They were surrounded by a huge crowd of people who were all smiling and waving and clapping.

Griff was astonished. The crowd, the man in the uniform and the Queen herself were all delighted with this goat. He was really something special. Griff felt a tinge of jealousy. Could there possibly be another goat who was more important than Griff? Griff was beginning to feel not just unhappy, but miserable. Everything had clearly gone very well for this goat in the photograph. Why had things gone so wrong for Griff? He looked more closely at the goat in the photograph. Yes, he was handsome with fine horns, but Griff was sure that he would look just as good if he was dressed up in such a splendid robe and headdress.

I'd probably look better, he thought. He glanced at the headline: "Gethin the Royal Taff Regimental goat dies peacefully after a long, happy and fulfilling career. Goat Major seeks new mascot from Snowdonia mountain herd."

It took Griff a few seconds to absorb this information. The Royal Taff Regiment needed a new goat mascot. They were coming to Snowdonia to find one. All his unhappiness and loneliness melted away in an instant. Hope gripped him.

Griff knew that he was perfect for the job. All he had to do was pose up on his rock until he was spotted. He was already famous anyway so everybody knew that he would be the chosen one! He would look superb in the robe and headdress!

He began to dream about the glorious parades

and adoration of the crowd, his luxurious quarters and all the hay and treats. He would have his very own pen to sleep in and a goat major to groom him and fuss him and love him! He would get to meet prime ministers and royalty!

The Goat Major could be here any minute! He needed to look his best. He looked up and suddenly noticed an army truck parked further along the lane. There was no time to lose! The Goat Major was here already! He may already have chosen his next goat mascot without even seeing Griff first! Bully Goat Griff set off up the mountain as fast as he could. He needed to be on that rock, showing off his magnificence!

– CHAPTER EIGHT –
Hopeful Goat

Griff didn't stop running until he reached the rock. When he got there he was shocked to discover that his rock was already occupied by another goat, and not only that, but there was a long

line of goats waiting patiently for their turn to stand upon the rock and be inspected by what must have been the Goat Major.

A group of soldiers stood nearby. One of them was holding a halter with shiny buckles.

Griff wasn't quite sure what to do for a moment. Should he join the long queue of hopeful goats? He didn't think that would be dignified or necessary for a goat of his superiority. He glanced up to see which ridiculous little goat had climbed up onto his rock to be viewed. Griff couldn't believe it. There was Kev the Kid standing up on his rock, and to add insult to injury, Kev had stolen Griff's pose! His head was turned up to the sky. His front hooves were symmetrically positioned together. He then lifted his skinny little right leg and held that pose for a few seconds. Instead of stamping his foot down, however, he brought it down gently.

Hah! thought Griff. *He can't even stamp his hoof!*

Griff had seen enough. He gave a loud snort. All the goats in the queue turned and as soon as they recognised Griff they bleated with surprise, shock and fear and then quickly dispersed in various directions across the mountain. Kev was the only other goat left, still posing on the rock. Griff lunged towards him and he dived off just in time and galloped away in clouds of dust.

The Goat Major didn't move. He stared at Griff who had now taken up his pose upon the rock. The Goat Major folded his arms. Griff turned his head down to look at him. He didn't look happy, but Griff was sure that he looked impressed. Griff returned his gaze up to the sky and raised his right hoof.

'Don't move!' commanded the Goat Major. Griff was startled. He wasn't used to being given orders. He had always been the boss. He felt confused and nervous. He didn't dare stamp his hoof, so he remained in the pose with his one foot held up. He didn't usually hold this pose for more than a few seconds and he was beginning to feel a bit wobbly, but he was desperate to impress. The Goat Major walked all around him slowly.

I really cannot hold onto this pose much longer, Griff thought. The Goat Major snapped another command.

'At ease!'

With relief, Griff brought his foot back down. He also turned his head to look at the group of soldiers to check that none of them were smirking.

'Head up!' barked the Goat Major. Griff instantly obeyed and returned his gaze to the skies.

He looked so much nicer in the photo, Griff thought. The Goat Major summoned one of the soldiers to bring him a clipboard.

'Right. This must be the famous Bully Goat Griff then,' he said.

Ah, thought Griff. *I'm so famous. Even the Goat Major knows me. Getting this job will be a doddle.*

'Hmm.' The Goat Major held the clipboard in one hand and a pencil in the other. 'Size… perfect. Coat condition… excellent…' He was ticking off boxes. 'Hooves… nicely shaped. Horns… beautiful. Posture… magnificent.' Griff felt awesome. Nobody had said anything so positive about him for a long, long time.

'Right. Good,' said the Goat Major. 'Griff, you are

a fantastic looking goat. So far, so good.'

What more could he possibly want to know? thought Griff. *I'm perfect and that's it. Just give me the job.* But the Goat Major went on.

'OK. Character and personality check. 'Is he friendly towards children?'... no. 'Friendly towards adults?'... no. 'Is he patient?'... no. 'Is he calm and gentle?'... no. 'Is he polite?'... no. 'Willing to learn?'... unlikely. 'Has he ever shown any signs of aggression?'... frequently.'

Griff could hear the sound of crosses being etched onto the clipboard. He was then utterly shocked when the Goat Major suddenly leapt up into the air and shouted, '**BOOOOOOO**!' so loudly it nearly blasted his ear drums.

Griff leapt off the rock, bleated with terror and was left shaken and uncertain what to do. His immediate reaction was to run away, but he was Bully Goat Griff and it would make him look silly. He stood his ground instead. The Goat Major looked down at his clipboard.

'Reaction to noise'... not bad. Hmm.'

He looked at Griff and sighed. He looked so deeply into Griff's eyes that Griff felt some sort of longing and connection, but he also felt uncomfortable. He was being judged. For the first time in his life, Griff didn't feel quite so confident anymore. It was the same feeling he had felt when Mrs Evans-Williams-Jenkins-Jones had belittled him. It was a confused feeling. An uncertain emotion.

'Well, Griff. You've got the looks I have to say, but as far as personality and character goes, well I'm sorry to say that I am unable to offer you the position of Goat Mascot to the Royal Taff Regiment.'

Griff's heart sank. How could anyone reject him? Why couldn't the Goat Major see how fabulous he really was? He had been so certain that the Goat Major was one of the few people in the world who really understood him, and would want him and need him as the new goat mascot.

He was too stunned to even snort in protest. He thought about turning away quickly and going off in a strut to fume and sulk somewhere, but something held him back. He needed to listen to what Goat Major Morgan had to say even though he suspected it wasn't going to be what he wanted to hear.

'I need a goat mascot that I can depend upon to always behave under all circumstances,' Goat Major Morgan explained. 'I need a goat who is friendly to everyone, young, old and everyone in between. I need a goat who is patient and calm and willing to train hard. Being a goat mascot isn't about being pompous and arrogant and seeking your own glory. It's about humble service and proudly representing your regiment and leading them out in front for very special occasions. I'm sorry, Griff. I can see you're keen, but no one likes a bully. If you want real respect and admiration, then you will have to earn it. You must change your ways. Now if you don't mind, I've plenty of other goats to inspect.'

That was it. Goat Major Morgan had nothing more to say to Griff. He just folded his arms and waited for Griff to leave. Griff stood in disbelief and shock gawping at the Goat Major.

'I haven't got all day, Griff, thank you.'

Griff turned and walked slowly away down the mountain. He turned his head back to look at Goat Major Morgan and made a feeble attempt to bleat pitifully hoping that Goat Major Morgan's heart would melt, and he would change his mind. He knew that Kev often won people's affection like this, but the Goat Major wasn't falling for it. In fact, he was no longer even looking at Griff. His eyes were back on his clip board and Griff could see his pencil crossing something out on the page.

My name... me... he's crossing me out, thought Griff.

He felt a sudden surge of anger. Perhaps he should show Goat Major Morgan exactly what he thought of him?! Goat Major Morgan deserved to feel the tip of his horns! But the next moment, Griff just felt sad and embarrassed and silly, and he couldn't bear to be there any minute longer. He wanted to get as far away from anyone as possible. Griff wanted to be alone. He felt more than belittled this time. He felt ashamed.

– CHAPTER NINE –
Hiding Goat

The following morning Griff stood hidden behind a tree and watched a long line of tourists beginning their ascent up the mountain. He wondered which goat had been chosen for the job of the new goat mascot. Maybe Adorable Alan? Tickly Terence? Galivanting Gareth? Happy Hywel maybe? Sniffy Sam? Dawdling Dan? He then noticed Kev the Kid begin to climb up close to the rock to greet all the visitors.

At least Kev didn't get the job, thought Griff. He knew the jealousy would have been unbearable. Griff saw Kev look up at the rock and then start to look around. He watched Kev wander a little way back down the mountain before heading back up again to the rock.

Go on then, scrawny little show off, thought Griff with a sniff. *Now that you've checked that I'm not around you might as well jump up onto my rock and start posing and looking for lots of attention. They don't want to see me anymore anyway. It's you they love now.*

Kev didn't jump up on to the rock. He just kept looking around as if he was searching for something. When the tourists arrived at the fence, Kev slowly wandered up to them and gave a few gentle bleats. He was patted and fussed and was offered some tasty snacks. Everyone was smiling and laughing and taking photos of Kev and having a lovely time.

Kev was adorable and loved. Every now and then Kev would turn around, as if he was still looking for something, before turning back to the crowd to relish further attention. Griff sighed. He was puzzled. Why did they love Kev so much?

What's he got that I haven't? pondered Griff.

Kev gratefully received a final offering of a juicy, red apple from a kind Welsh tourist.

'Mae hynny'n dda, ie?' ('That's good, yes?') said the tourist, scratching Kev's nose in exactly the spot

where Kev loved to be scratched most. Kev closed his eyes utterly content and bleated in gratitude. Griff was fascinated. What must it be like to have your nose scratched gently like that? It must be so blissful. He decided that he wanted to let people scratch his nose too, but with everyone being so afraid of him, that was highly unlikely ever to happen. Griff sighed sadly.

Kev came out of his trance like state and opened his eyes. The tourist patted his head and said, '*Rwy ti'n hyfryd, ond wyt ti?*' ('You're lovely, aren't you?') before turning away to continue the climb.

Kev turned away too and began to walk away from the group of visitors. He knew that Griff was watching him. Griff was a large goat and had no idea that his rear was completely visible on one side of the tree trunk and that his horns stuck out quite a bit on the other side.

Kev was concerned that Griff had failed for the first time ever to make his daily appearance. He knew how heartbroken Griff must have felt after being rejected for the position of goat mascot the previous day. Once he had spotted Griff hiding behind the tree, however, he knew this was the perfect opportunity to show Griff how a good goat ought to behave. He knew that none of the other goats had been chosen so far and that Griff still had the opportunity to shine and get the job, if only he could change his behaviour in time. He was also aware that Goat Major Morgan was hiding behind another tree a few hundred metres away watching Griff through binoculars.

– CHAPTER TEN –

Reflective Goat

Kev started to make his way back down the mountain and he deliberately walked very close to the tree where Griff was hiding. As Kev was about to pass by, Griff suddenly stepped out and blocked his path. Griff wasn't quite sure why he'd done that. It was just the sort of intimidating thing that he had got into the habit of doing.

Kev though didn't seem surprised or startled or concerned or even slightly intimidated. He simply looked up at Griff with questioning eyes. Griff began an attempt to stare him out.

Kev broke off the eye contact quickly however and looked further up into the sky. What had caught Kev's eye? Griff couldn't resist looking up too. They both gazed for a minute or so at a bright, red balloon that was floating high across the sky with the string still attached.

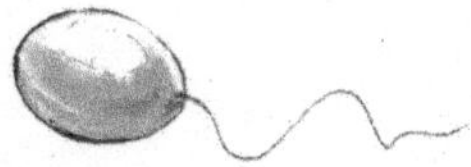

They could hear the distant wail of a small child at the bottom of the mountain. Griff recognised the wail.

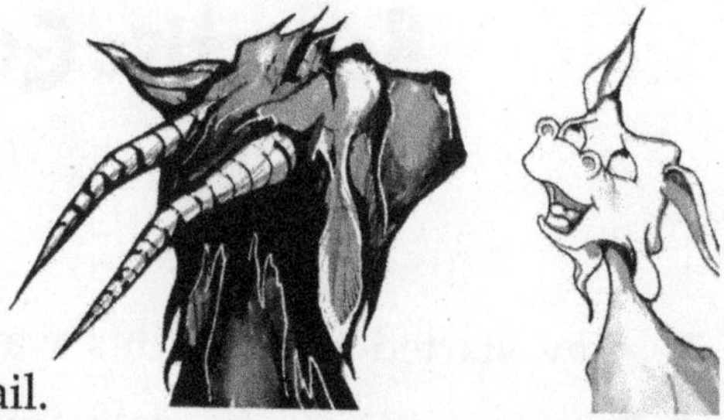

He'd heard it before. It was the sound of little Sioni Siencyns. He must have been to another party in the village hall and had lost his balloon again. He didn't seem to have much luck with balloons.

Griff tried to remember something. Wasn't Sioni the one who had given him a delicious piece of cake? Yes, he was. Then he lost his balloon. No… wait. He didn't let go of it. He lost the balloon because… because… Griff had burst it! Little Sioni Siencyns had shared his cake with Griff, and then Griff had burst his beloved balloon in return!

Griff shuddered with a sense of regret and shame. *Why did I do that? Why was I so mean?* His behaviour that day had been awful. It may have been fun for Griff to watch the balloon disappear with a bang, but for little Sioni it hadn't been fun at all. It had made him cry. In fact, it had made him wail with sorrow. Griff then remembered the mother's words. '*Bwli wyt ti!*' ('You're a bully!')

Griff's mind was suddenly spinning with all the other occasions that he had hurt or upset anyone. There were an awful lot of occasions to think about. He had been unkind and rude and spiteful and selfish so many times!

Maybe that was what Goat Major Morgan had been talking about when he said Griff wasn't friendly to people? Griff snapped out of his thoughts, suddenly remembering that Kev was right there and probably gloating over Griff's shame and downfall. There was nothing worse than a gloating goat, especially when it was Kev the Kid. Griff looked down but Kev had disappeared. Kev always knew when to disappear. Griff glanced down the mountain and spotted him again. Kev was heading down to the cottage where Mrs Evans-Williams-

Jenkins-Jones lived.

Well, you won't get any love or treats there anymore. If I can't get over that huge wall, then there's no way a puny little goat like you can get into the garden.

Nevertheless, Griff was beginning to feel a bit of respect for Kev the Kid. Kev was clever and had probably managed to find a way into the garden, and this could be very useful.

Griff followed Kev down towards the cottage. There may not be a basket full of goodies on her doorstep anymore, but there was certainly a garden full of lush, gorgeous, mouth-watering delights.

Griff imagined getting into the garden once more and chomping on all the flowers and bushes. The blueberry bushes were always so tempting. Didn't he get his horns stuck in a blueberry bush once? Yes, he had. That was the day Mrs Evans-Williams-Jenkins-Jones had suddenly turned very cold and nasty towards Griff and all the other goats. Not long after that she had her garden wall built higher to keep them all out. That was surely because of the thief that made off with her pagoda though... or was it?

Griff then remembered what he had done to Mrs Evans-Williams-Jenkins-Jones. He had butted her because he had been angry. After all her kindness and generosity over the years, he had repaid her with a significant butt in the rear. She had the wall built up higher after that to stop all the goats going into her garden for afternoon treats. He had spoilt everything for everyone. No wonder Goat Major Morgan didn't want him as the new goat mascot.

Griff now fully understood how awful he had been. Having the title 'Bully Goat Griff' wasn't an honour, as he had once thought. None of the other goats liked him anymore. None of the tourists were interested in him and he had been rejected by the Royal Taff Regiment. Even Mrs Evans-Williams-Jenkins-Jones, the loveliest lady in the whole of Wales who loved all goats, didn't love *him* anymore. To say that Griff was feeling rather negative about himself was an understatement. Griff's world had now totally collapsed, and he felt hopelessly ashamed and depressed.

– CHAPTER ELEVEN –
Changed Goat

When Griff reached the cottage of Mrs Evans-Williams-Jenkins-Jones, he discovered much to his surprise that the gates were unlocked and wide open. There was a lorry parked further up the road, close to the high wall. He peeped cautiously inside the garden through the open gates and spotted Kev the Kid on the lawn being hugged and patted and scratched on his nose by little Sioni Siencyns.

Little Sioni's face was still wet with tears having accidentally let go of his latest balloon from his latest party (young children go to a lot of parties), but he was very happy now. Kev the Kid was cheering him up and getting a slice of birthday cake for his reward.

Griff was jealous for a few seconds but then, quite unexpectedly, forgot about being jealous and actually started feeling glad that little Sioni wasn't upset anymore. Kev was doing such a good job helping Sioni to feel better, and Griff began to enjoy watching the two together.

Griff didn't move into the garden as he knew that Sioni would be frightened if he saw him. He didn't want Sioni to feel upset or frightened. He wanted Sioni to feel happy and safe. Kev was happy too and Griff didn't want to spoil things. Griff began to feel very proud of himself for not wanting to spoil things. It was a nice feeling, not being awful for a change.

Griff then noticed two men carrying a large garden pagoda and being directed by Mrs Evans-Williams-Jenkins-Jones to an empty spot at the other end of the garden.

'Down by there will be fine, thank you,' Mrs Evans-Williams-Jenkins-Jones instructed the men. Griff wondered why she wasn't having it put in the same place as before to cover up the bare patch of earth where her previous pagoda had stood, but he then noticed that another new garden pagoda had already been positioned over the bare patch of earth.

Two pagodas? He was very puzzled. He watched Mrs Evans-Williams-Jenkins-Jones and Sioni's mother as they stood looking at the newest pagoda and chatting cheerfully together.

'Well there's lovely it looks by there,' said Sioni's mother. 'Really lovely. Very, very lovely.'

'Yes. Well, I'm beginning to run out of space now,' replied Mrs Evans-Williams-Jenkins-Jones. 'I'm not sure there's room for many more.'

More? thought Griff. He looked around the garden. There was another pagoda in position by the blueberry bushes. *Three*... he began counting... another one by the green house. *Four*... another one by the fruit trees. *Five*. He was intrigued.

The delivery men were now walking back

towards the gates and so he quickly darted into the garden and hid in the shadows. The men walked past, out through the gates and into the road. He heard them crunching their way back up the road, laughing.

'Doniol iawn!' ('Very funny!') said one, chuckling to the other. Griff then heard the lorry doors being slammed shut and the engine spluttering loudly into life. No one had noticed that Griff was in the garden.

Well, I'm in now, so I may as well take a look, he thought, and he silently slipped around the cottage and into to the back garden. *Six... seven... eight... nine... ten!*

He was perplexed. He couldn't understand why Mrs Evans-Williams-Jenkins-Jones had ordered ten pagodas. Why was she hoarding pagodas? Perhaps she missed all the goats so much that she had begun to replace them all with pagodas? It was just bizarre. Having one garden pagoda was very nice, but ten was going a bit overboard surely?

As Griff was trying to work out the reason for the abundance of pagodas in the garden, he heard the lorry's engine getting louder as it was heading down the hill from the top of the road. He quickly returned to the front garden.

Little Sioni Siencyns was laughing loudly and clapping his hands with delight. Kev the Kid's face was covered in fresh cream and it was very funny. Little Sioni then began to skip around the garden.

'Tyrd ymlaen, Kev!' ('Come on, Kev!') Sioni shouted playfully. He was skipping towards the open garden gate.

Griff could hear the van's engine getting louder and louder. It had picked up speed and was about to drive past the gates.

At that very moment, little Sioni skipped out of the gates, straight into the road and into the path of the lorry! Kev bleated in terror! Sioni's mother screamed in horror! Mrs Evans-Williams-Jenkins-Jones, as we know, was nimble, flexible and fast… but not nimble, flexible and fast enough to reach Sioni in time!

Griff, however, was.

Within a split second he leaped over the lawn and out into the road, placing himself between little Sioni Siencyns and the oncoming lorry.

There was a horrendous screeching of breaks. For one moment in time, lasting no more than a tenth of a second, Griff was staring the driver of the lorry right in the eye. This wasn't his usual glare or stare of aggression though. This was a stare of fear, of pleading for the child's life. Griff was willing to sacrifice his own life to save the child. It was instinctive. It was the only thing he could do. It had to be done. Griff quickly shut his eyes and waited for the end.

– CHAPTER TWELVE –

Heroic Goat

Halfway up the mountain Goat Major Morgan lowered his binoculars. He had witnessed everything.

'I knew there was something extraordinary about you, Griff.' He had been spying on Griff ever since he had turned him down for the job of goat mascot for the Royal Taff Regiment the day before. He nodded to himself and made his way back down the mountain.

Meanwhile, back at the bottom of the mountain, outside the gates of Mrs Evans-Williams-Jenkins-Jones's cottage, Griff opened his eyes.

He had felt the lorry thud against his head and had heard glass smashing, followed by an enormous cracking sound. He was now staring into the face of the shocked lorry driver.

The windscreen had shattered, and the lorry driver's mouth was wide open in shock. Griff could see that the driver had at least seven fillings and very smelly breath. He wondered if he ever cleaned his teeth properly. He wrinkled his nose in disgust.

He then realised what had caused the enormous cracking sound; his left horn was dangling down, barely still attached. Yesterday this would have caused Griff some serious anxiety and anger issues, but today it was little more than a pity. The only real thing that mattered today was that little Sioni Siencyns was now being cradled and *cwtched* (cuddled) in his grateful mother's arms, having narrowly escaped a dreadful disaster.

Mrs Evans-Williams-Jenkins-Jones insisted that everyone should have a strong cup of tea to get over the shock and went inside to boil the kettle. The delivery driver and his assistant shakily got out of the lorry and went to sit down on the garden chairs, shaking their heads and wiping away sweat and tears. Sioni's mother turned to Griff, as she still held her child tightly.

'Griff,' she said. *'Arwr wyt ti.* (You're a hero) *Diolch.* (Thank you)' She bent forward and softly kissed Griff on his head. Griff had never received such affection from anyone before and he felt all tingly and nice. She then gently took hold of the horn that was only just still attached to Griff's head, in the hope that she could somehow pop it back into place. Unfortunately, though, it came away in her hand and there was nothing she could do to save it.

'Awww. Trueni. (A pity.) *Mae'n ddrwg gen i, Griff,* (Sorry, Griff,)' she said.

At that moment little Sioni reached for the horn. Griff turned his head to one side in an attempt to look cute and he bleated gently. He wanted little Sioni to have the horn.

'Dyna ti, cariad, (There you are, love,)' said Mrs Siencyns allowing her son to hold the horn. Little

Sioni's eyes sparkled with delight and he clutched it tight as his mother carried him back into the garden.

Griff stood there, stunned. He began to imagine his new life as a one-horned goat. It would be... different.

Kev came out through the gates and looked up at Griff. He'd never seen a one-horned goat before, and he was fascinated. Griff certainly looked different. Mrs Evans-Williams-Jenkins-Jones then appeared carrying a basket full of fruit and vegetables and plonked it at Griff's feet.

'Griff,' she said, 'You were incredible just then. I have never seen such agility. I am most impressed.

You are a different goat today than you were a few weeks back when... well, we all know what happened a few weeks back but we shan't dwell on it. I have forgiven you. You have redeemed yourself. Rest assured that you and all your friends may enter through my garden gates for afternoon munchies every teatime from now on. Griff, you are a magnificent goat on the outside and a truly remarkable goat on the inside.'

She patted Griff on his head before turning away and heading off back into the garden to pour the tea. Griff looked down at the basket of munchies. So did Kev. Griff allowed Kev to take the first bite, then both goats shared the tastiest basket of treats ever.

– CHAPTER THIRTEEN –

Adored Goat

Within a few days, news of Griff's heroic deed had spread throughout Wales and beyond. Journalists and tourists were swarming around the cottage of Mrs Evans-Williams-Jenkins-Jones each day from dawn to dusk. Copious amounts of tea was poured from the precious porcelain teapot and numerous slices of home-baked carrot cake were consumed. Griff posed for hundreds of photographs with Sioni holding the severed horn up triumphantly.

Mrs Evans-Williams-Jenkins-Jones enjoyed explaining to everyone the reason for her having acquired so many garden pagodas recently. The truth was out.

'Well, as you all know,' she said 'When my first pagoda was stolen, this lovely young budding journalist here wrote an article about the theft for the local newspaper and they liked the article so much, that they decided to print it. Have you got a copy of the article, Gwilym?'

'Yes, Mrs E.W.J.J.' replied the proud young journalist. 'I always keep a copy of it. I was given a permanent job as a journalist with the Snowdonia Weekly News after I wrote that article.'

Gwilym took out a battered newspaper cutting to show everyone. The article was all about the theft of the garden pagoda from the cottage of a local, gentle, dear and vulnerable little old lady who was adored by all the mountain goats.

Griff managed to get a glimpse of the photograph in the article and saw to his surprise a picture of Kev the Kid with Mrs 'E.W.J.J.' looking very sad, standing upon the bare patch of earth where the pagoda had once stood. Griff had no idea that Kev had become so famous in his own right after being in the newspaper all those weeks ago. He had just assumed that Kev had stolen the limelight off him after following him up the mountain each morning to greet the tourists.

'And you see,' continued Mrs Evans-Williams-Jenkins-Jones, 'Since the article was printed, there were rather a lot of very kind and generous garden centre owners who had taken it upon themselves to replace my stolen pagoda. I could hardly turn them away. That would have seemed so ungrateful. I mean it's such a kind gesture from each of them, so I just politely accepted them all. I only hope that no more arrive as the garden is getting a bit overcrowded.'

Griff looked around and counted at least fifteen more new pagodas, and that was just in the front garden. There were square pagodas, hexagonal pagodas and even some octagonal ones in every nook and cranny of the garden.

Well, that explains it, he thought.

It wasn't long before photographs of Griff, the one-horned heroic goat, appeared in just about every newspaper on the planet. Snowdonia thronged with more and more visitors who were all eager to catch a glimpse of both Kev and Griff together.

Griff returned to the rock each morning at eleven o'clock to pose alongside Kev.

They just about managed to fit onto the rock together. The fact that Griff now only had one horn actually made it a bit easier. After posing he always took time to meet and greet everyone just as Kev did. Griff was gentle and friendly and adored.

One thing puzzled him though. He often noticed a strange glint as the sun's light reflected on something higher up in the mountain. It seemed to catch his eye most mornings. He was sure that Kev noticed it as well, but Kev just ignored it. Griff began to feel more and more intrigued though.

One morning, about two weeks after he became a newspaper sensation, Griff saw the glint again and as soon as he had finished meeting and greeting the tourists, he decided it was time to investigate.

He climbed further up the mountain in the direction of the glint. He was getting closer. Eventually he arrived at a large bush, surrounded by small rocks. There was nothing there. He walked right around the bush. He bleated. Then, slowly, a beret began to appear from the middle of the bush.

Griff was astonished as he watched the head of Goat Major Morgan gradually emerge from the middle of the bush, followed by his shoulders, and then his body in full camouflage army uniform. Goat Major Morgan then stepped out of the bush. He was holding binoculars in one hand and a halter with shiny brass buckles in the other.

'Griff, I believe that you have become the most magnificent goat inside and out. If you are still interested, I would now like to offer you the position of Goat Mascot to the Royal Taff Regiment.'

Griff was stunned. He stared at the halter. It was beautiful. He was being offered his dream job. He thought about what he would be leaving behind. The last two weeks had been the best ever. All the goats in the herd were now his friends. All the tourists and locals loved him.

He knew though, that the tourist job now belonged to Kev. Kev was growing fast. He was no longer a kid. He was growing into a mature and magnificent mountain goat that all the visitors would flock to admire. Kev could pull in the punters without Griff. Now it was time to move into new pastures. Griff stepped forward and slipped his head into the halter.

'Perfect fit, Griff,' said Goat Major Morgan. The Goat Major then scratched Griff on his nose for a whole minute. It was bliss. The two then walked side by side down the mountain path together.

Goat Major Morgan had never known such a willing and obedient goat. It had taken a squad of ten soldiers two months of running up and down the mountain to catch Gethin, who at the time, hadn't been quite so keen on leaving the mountain herd.

Goat Major Morgan knew Griff would be easy to train and perfectly ready in time for his first official engagement. Goat Major Morgan had found his next best friend, and so had Griff.

– CHAPTER FOURTEEN –

New Goat Mascot

The moment had arrived. Goat Major Morgan looked down and into Griff's eyes.

'Ready, buddy?'

Griff nodded. He was ready. He could not have been more ready.

He had spent the last four months training hard. The discipline was tough, and each day had been a challenge on the parade ground in the barracks. However, the huge basket of tasty treats with fresh bales of hay each afternoon, and all the blissful nose scratches and heaps of praise and a huge sense of achievement, had made each challenging drill worth it. He could now march in perfect time. Nothing distracted him when he was on parade. Whatever sound or movement happened around him, he remained focused and professional.

Now he stood proudly in full ceremonial dress next to Goat Major Morgan who was standing to attention in his immaculate uniform. Griff's beautifully embroidered robe fitted snugly, and his shiny silver headdress was gleaming. Goat Major Morgan had even polished up Griff's horn for the occasion.

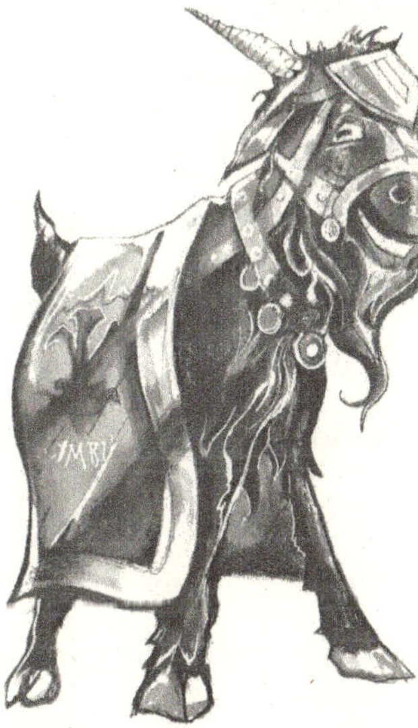

And what an occasion it was!

The brass band of the Royal Taff Regiment started to play, and over seventy thousand rugby fans cheered and roared as Griff, the magnificent goat mascot to the Royal Taff Regiment, led the parade and players out onto the pitch in the Principality Stadium. The parade reached the centre and then an astonishing hush fell upon all inside the stadium.

Griff and Goat Major Morgan had reached their marked position and now stood like statues with heads held high waiting. Griff was amazed at how *so* many people could be *so* quiet after being *so* noisy.

Then it happened. The band began once more to play, and the Welsh national anthem boomed out over Cardiff. Griff had never heard such an awesome sound. It was spine tingling. Hairs on the back of his neck stood up.

Without moving his head, he cast his eyes up to an immense screen and was amazed to see an enormous image of himself on television. The screen then changed to shots of the Welsh rugby team singing with great gusto and emotion. It then changed back to him again, and then to shots of various Welsh rugby fans waving flags and singing with great passion.

The screen shot went back to him again, this time with Goat Major Morgan and then onto Colonel Cadwaladr who was standing to attention, overcome with emotion, and in floods of tears. Griff could see that the colonel was desperate to wipe his nose and his moustache was quivering uncontrollably.

There were more shots of various fans singing their hearts out and then there was one that almost caused him to lose concentration. It was a brief shot lasting only a few seconds, but there was no doubt about who it was. There, with a porcelain teacup in one hand and waving a Welsh flag in the other, and singing triumphantly in between sips of tea, was Mrs Evans-Williams-Jenkins-Jones!

The camera then panned across and there was Gwilym the journalist busy scribbling down notes for his next article in the Snowdonia Weekly News, which would, of course, be all about Griff's first grand, ceremonial appearance.

Next to Gwilym, little Sioni Siencyns was being bounced up and down on his mother's knee. Sioni wasn't waving a flag though. He was waving Griff's missing left horn instead.

Griff had never felt so happy, so proud and so content. They would always be there with him forever, all those who had shown him how to be the best he could possibly, ever be.